Cursive Handwriting

for Kids

Children's Reading & Writing Education Books

BABY PROFESSOR

EDUCATION KIDS

Practice Writing

1
2
A
AIRPLANE
1
2

B
BOOK

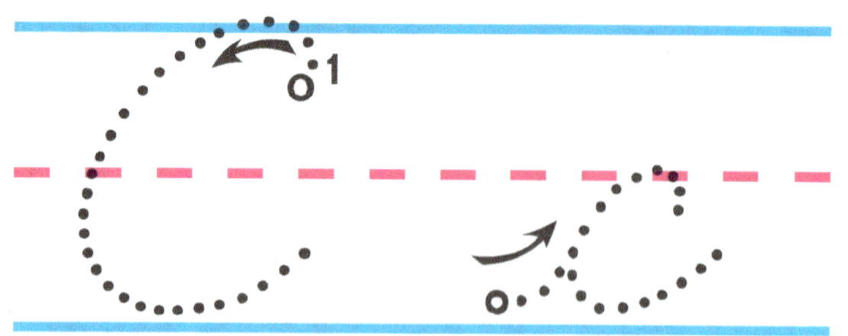

C

CHAMELEON

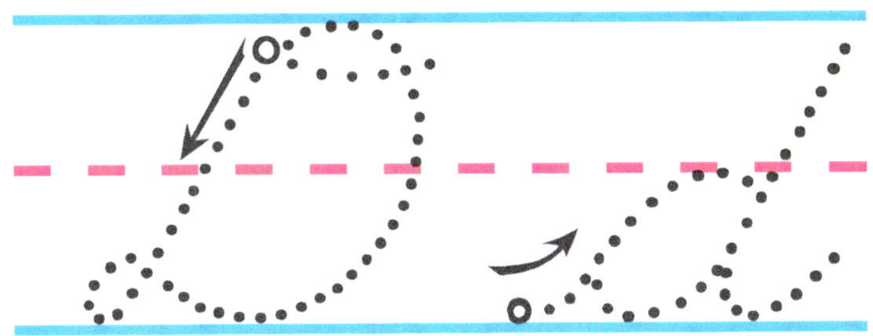

D

DRESS

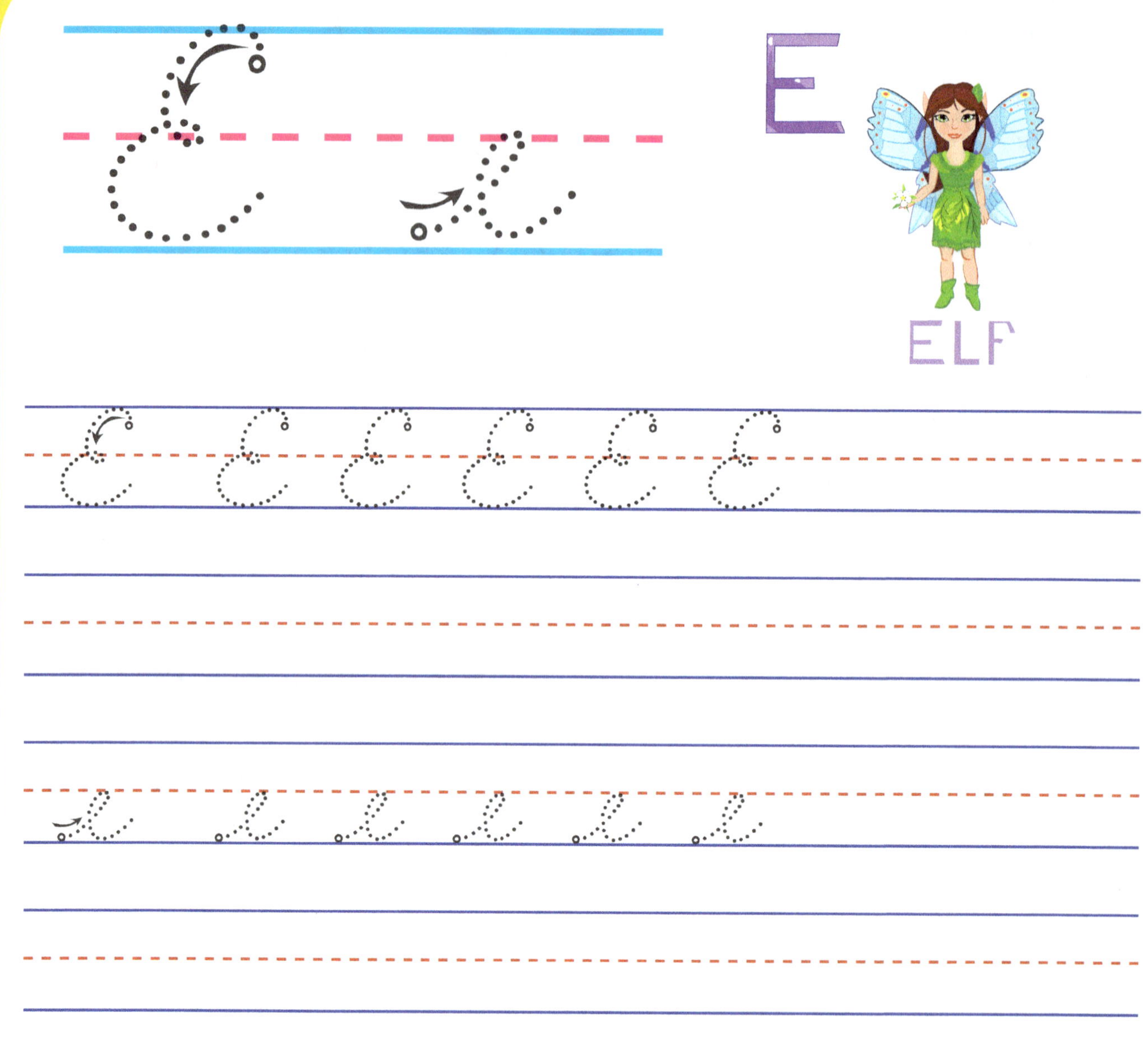

E

ELf

F

FROG

1
2
G
GIRAFFE

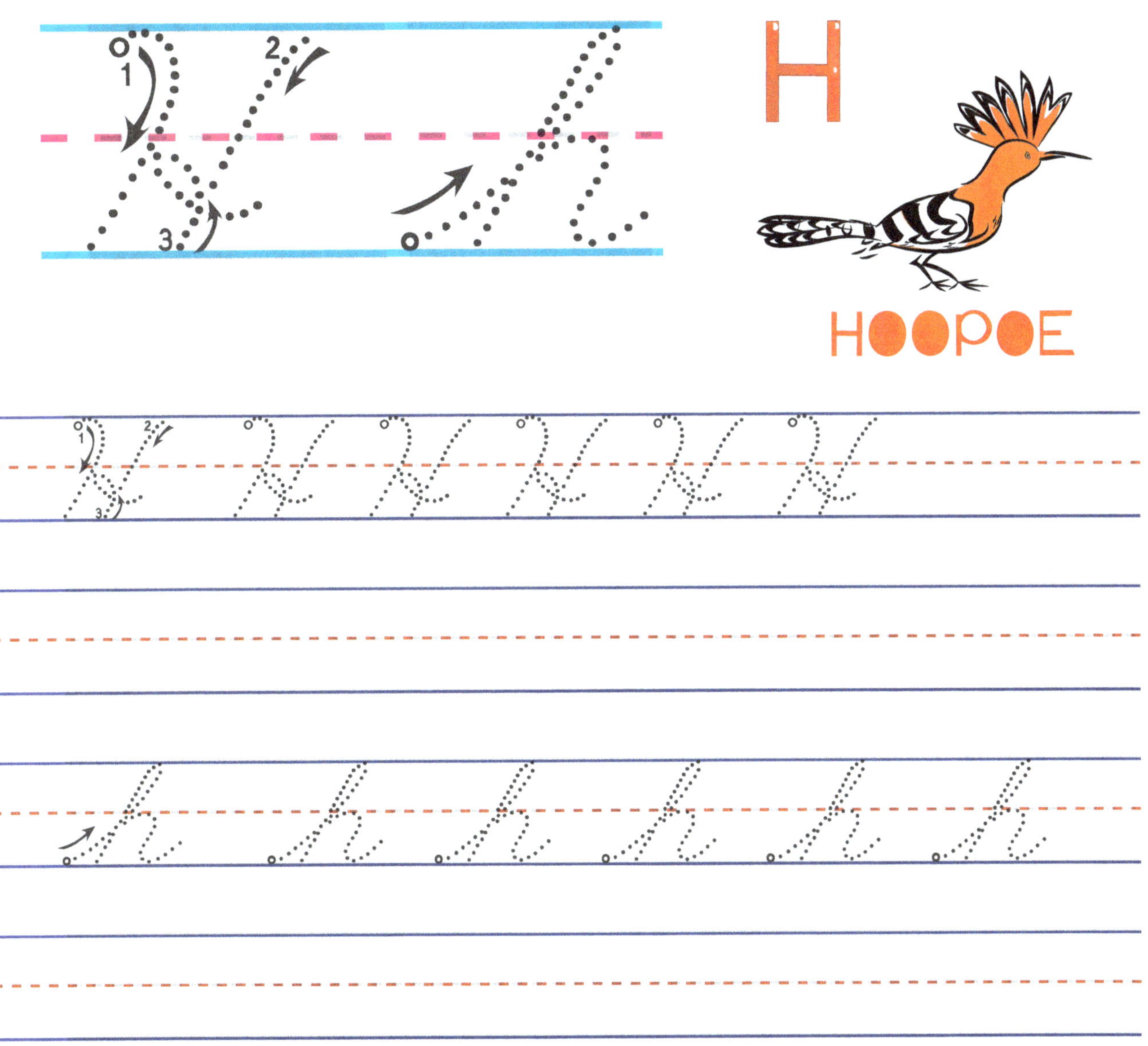

H
HOOPOE

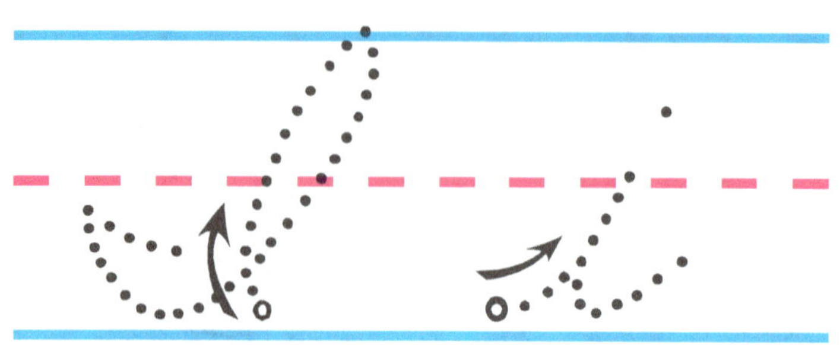

ISLAND

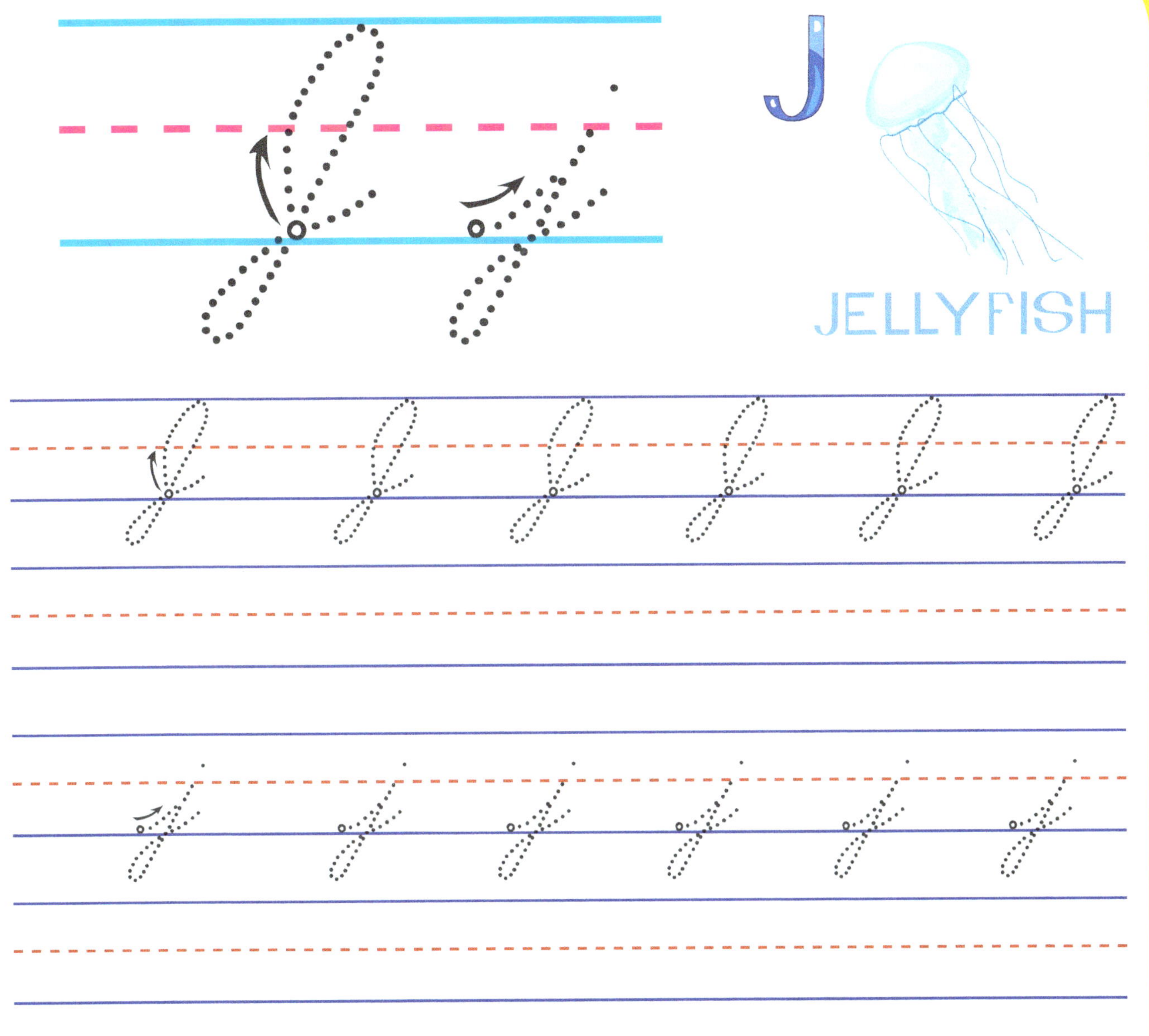

J
JELLYFISH

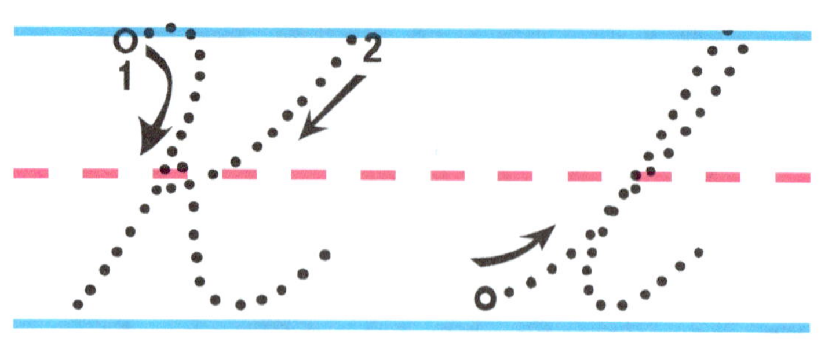

K

KANGAROO

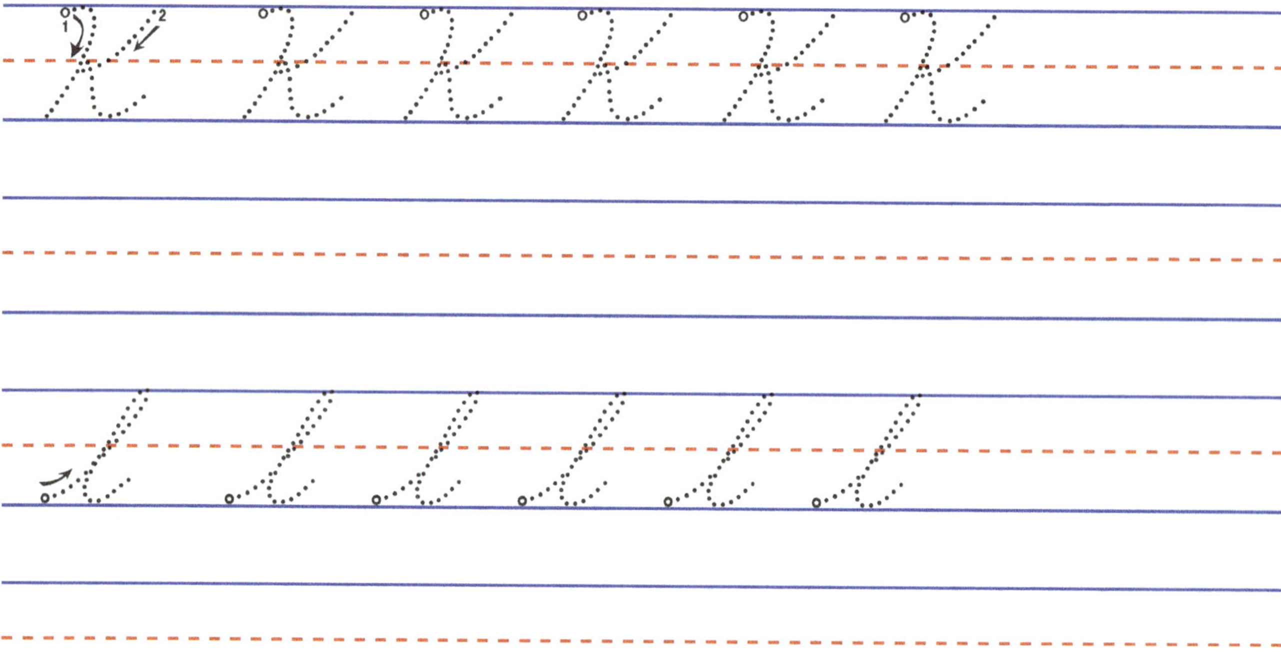

L

LIZARD

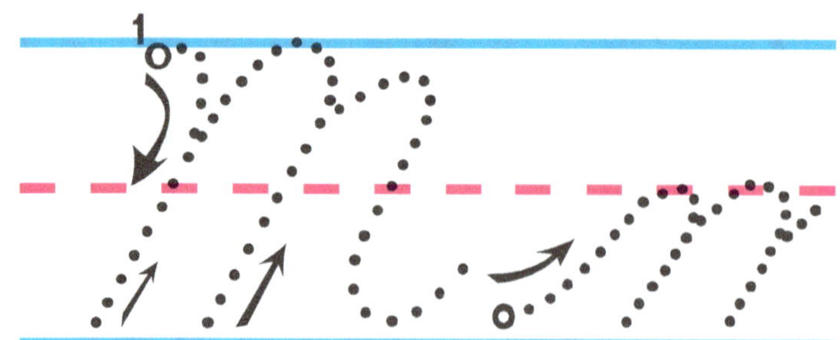

MUSHROOM

N

NUT

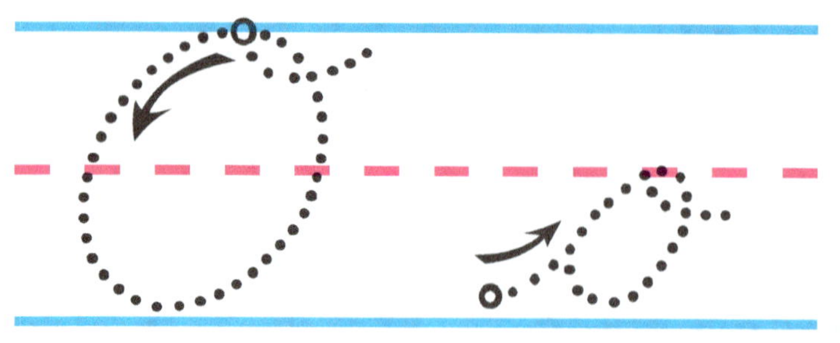

OCTOPUS

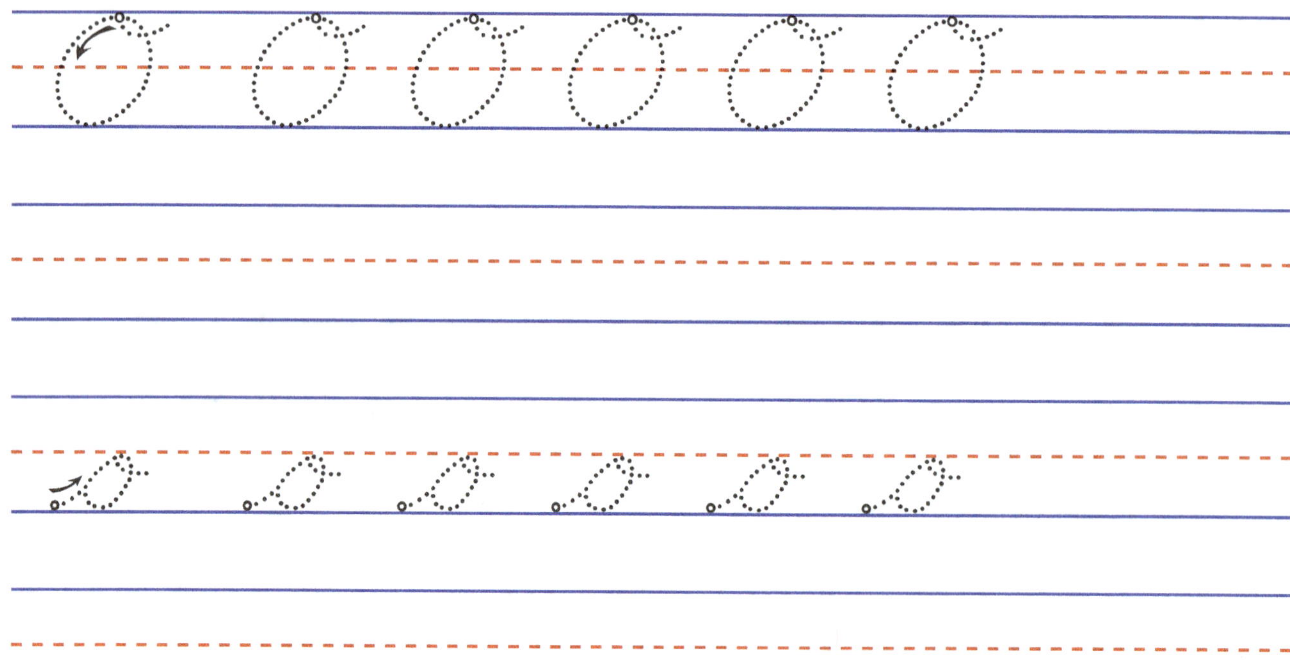

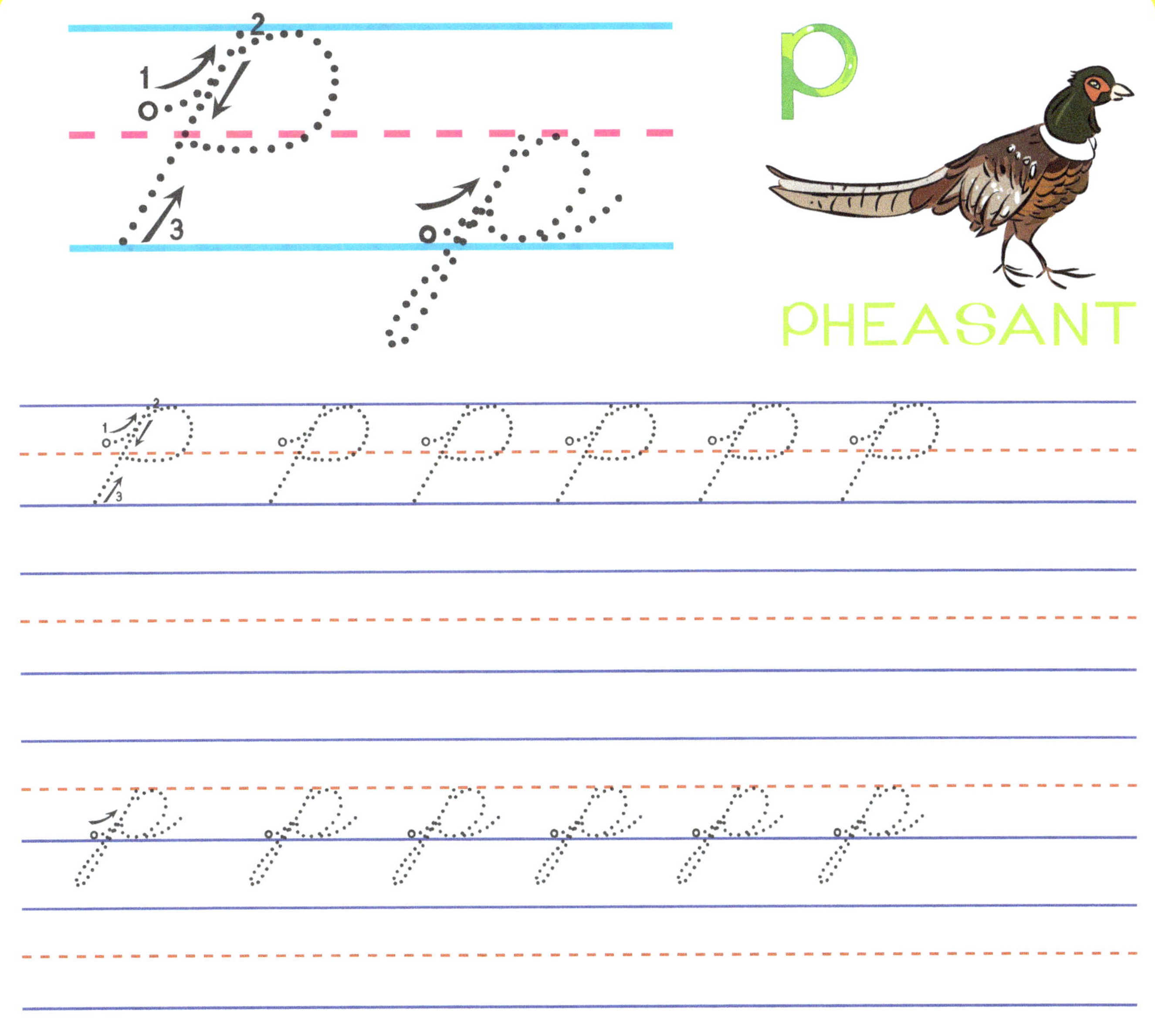

P p

PHEASANT

QUINCE

R
ROSE

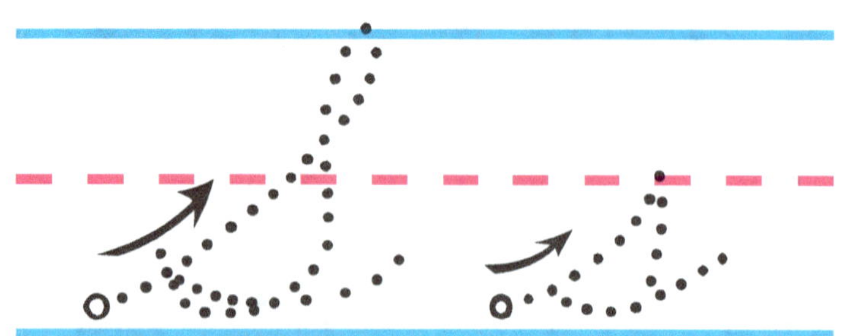

SPRUCE

T
TADPOLE

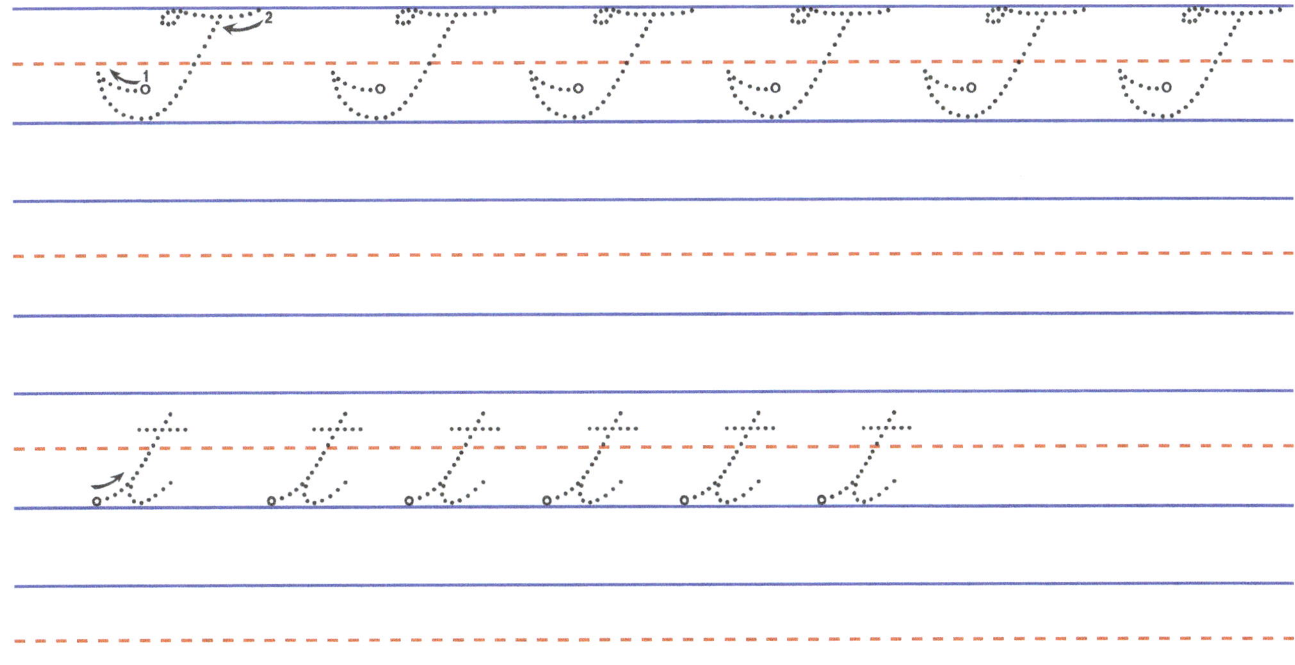

UMBRELLA

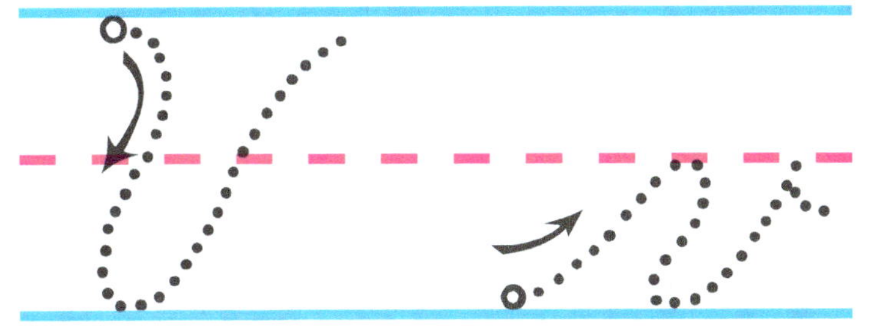

VAMPIRE BAT

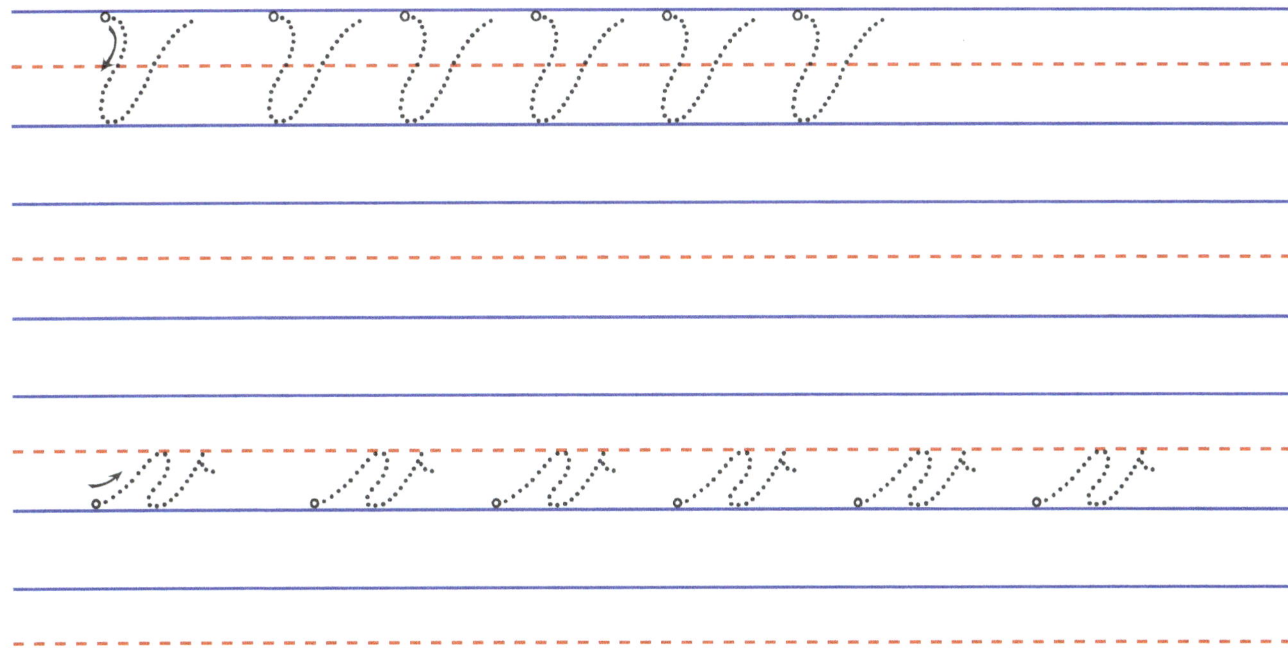

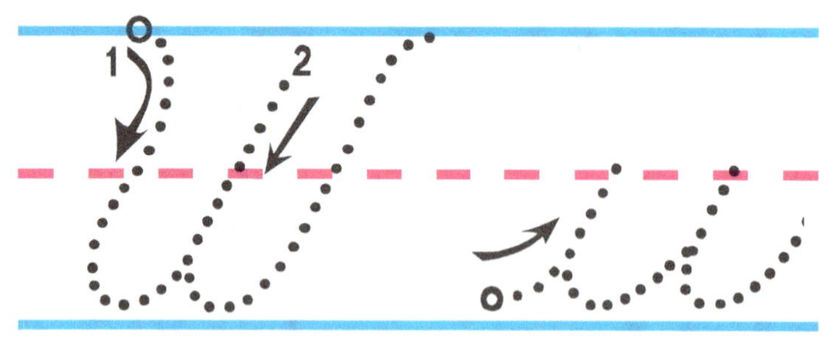

W

WATERMELON

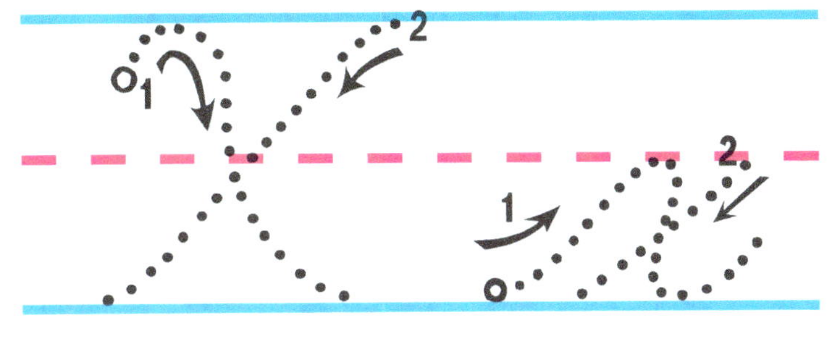

X-RAY FISH

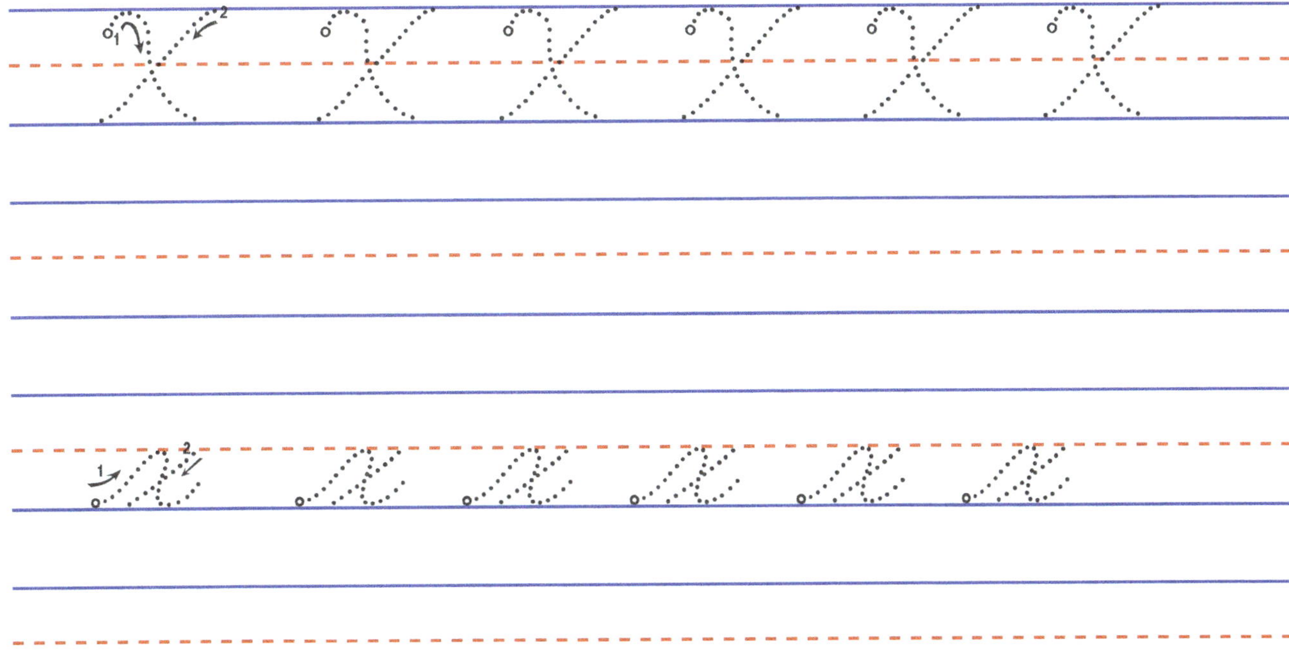

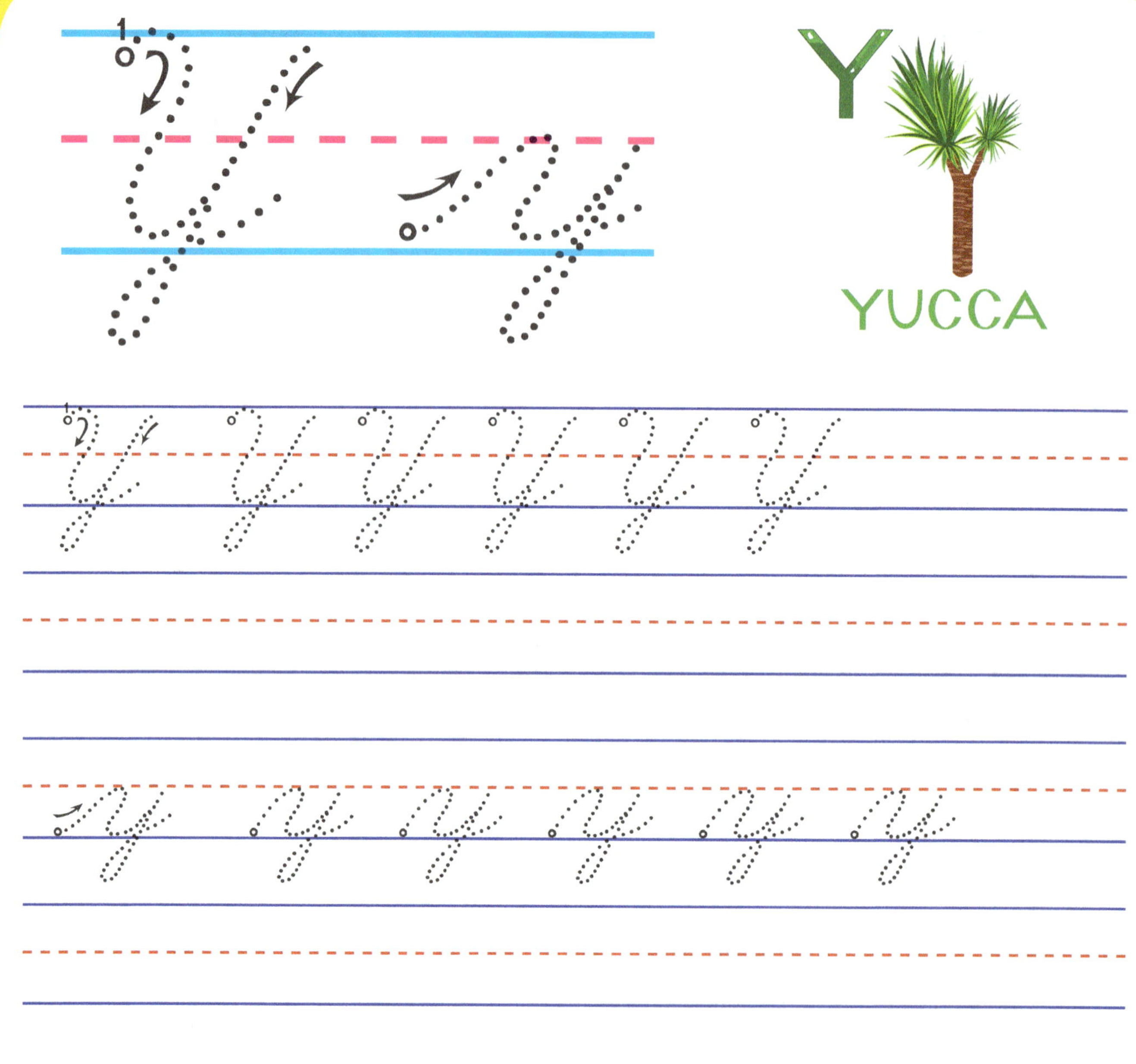

Y
YUCCA

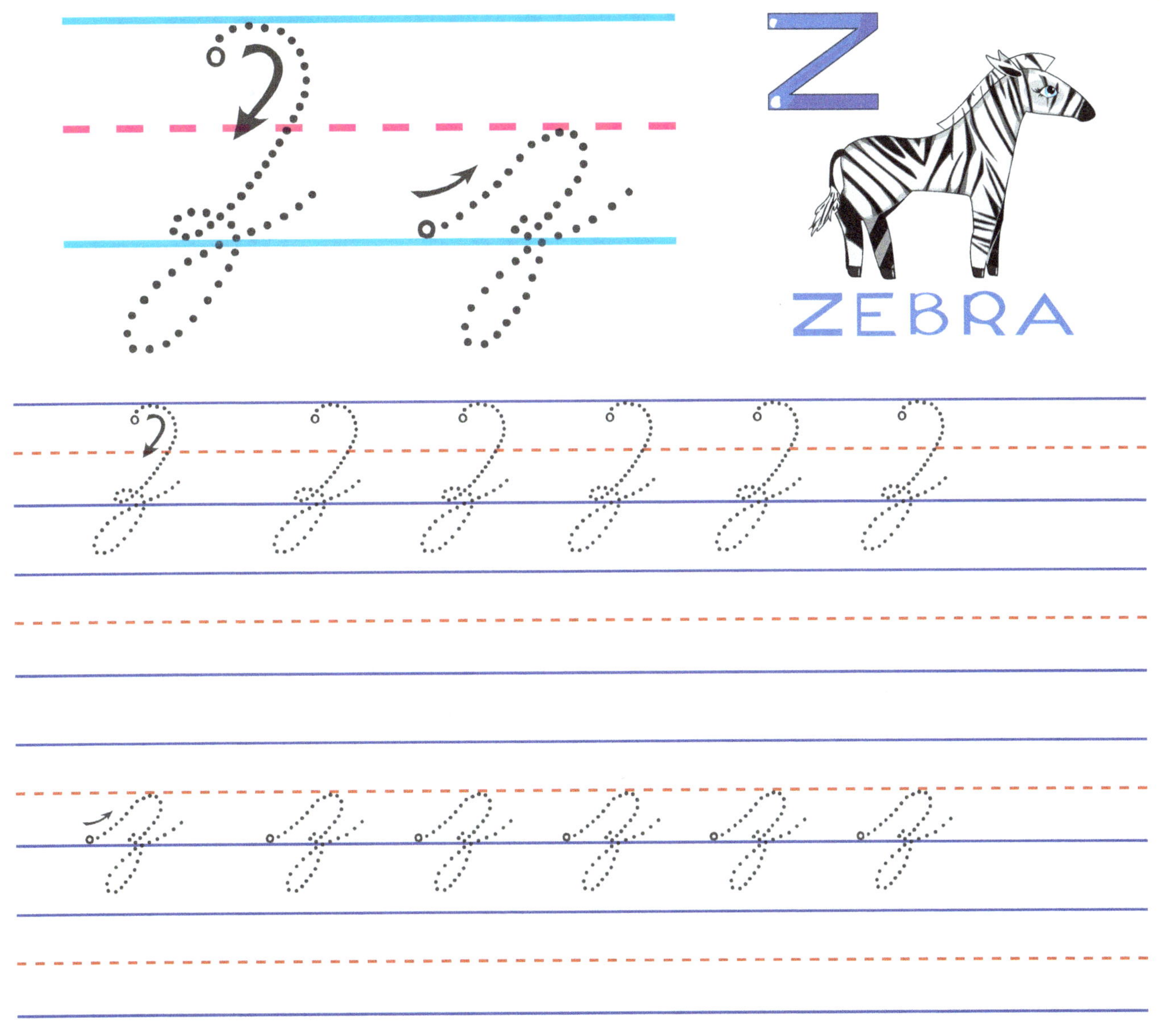

Z

ZEBRA

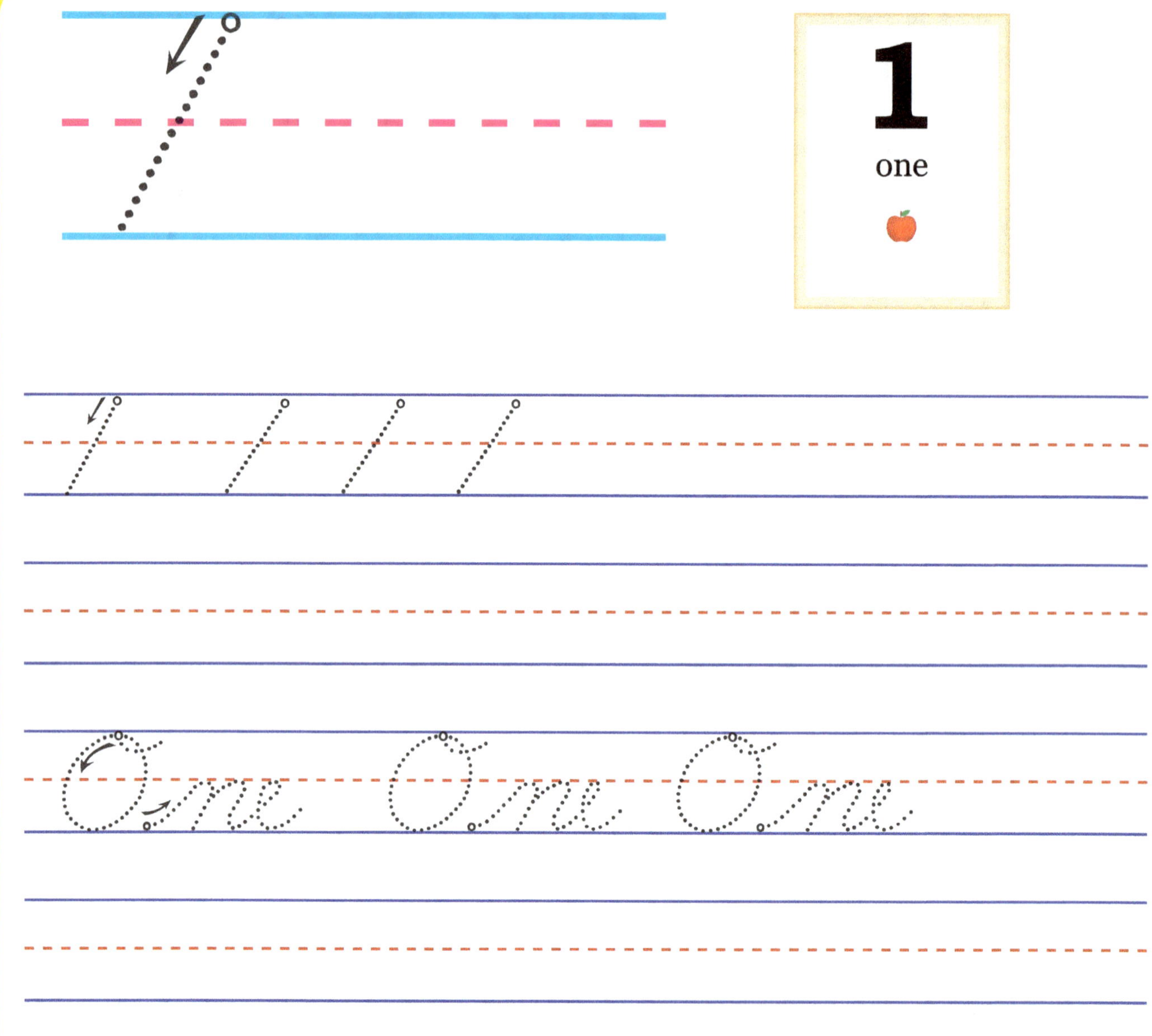

1
one

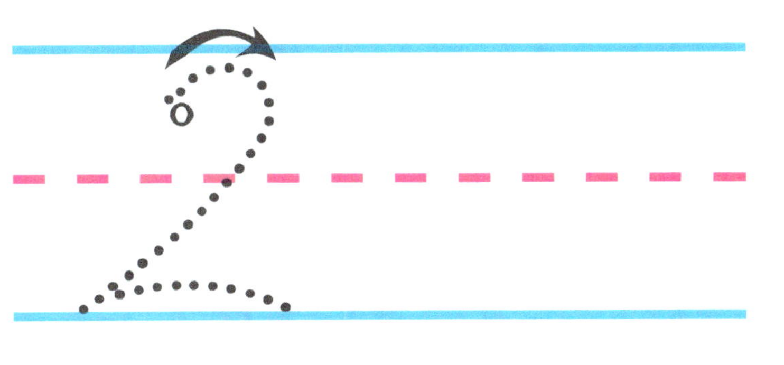

2
two

3
three

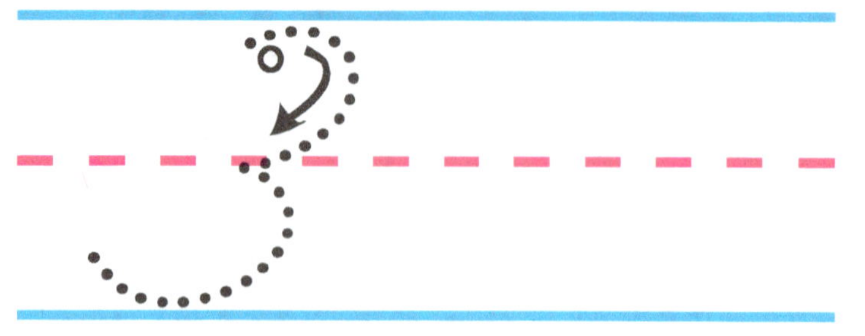

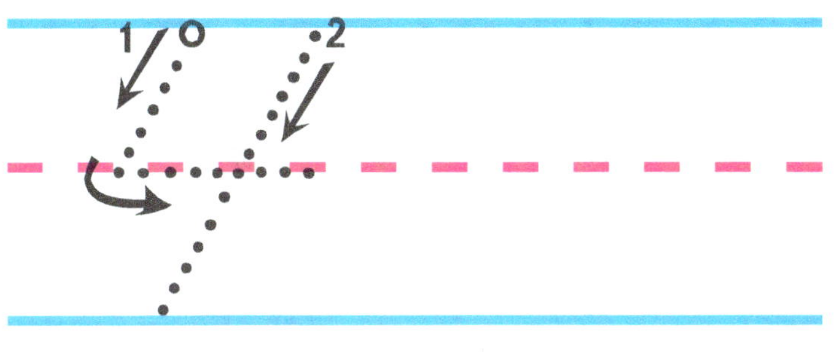

4

four

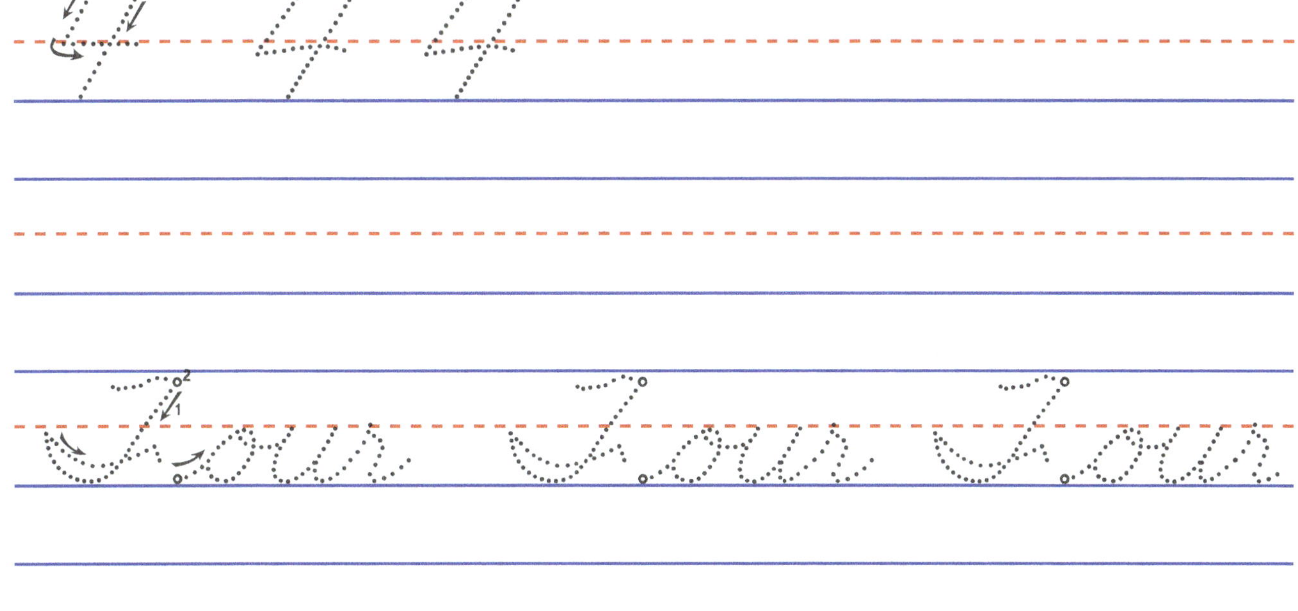

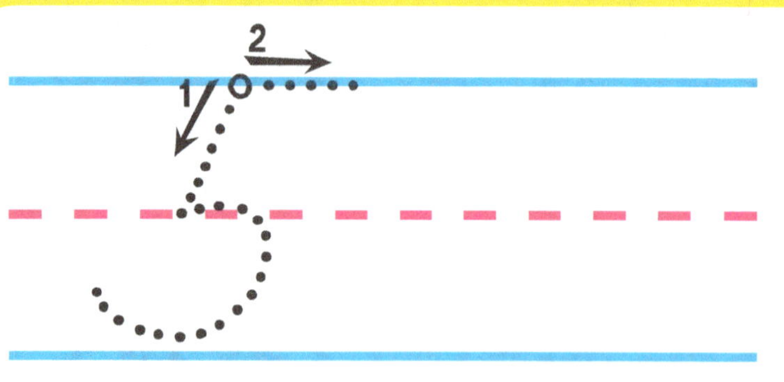

5
five

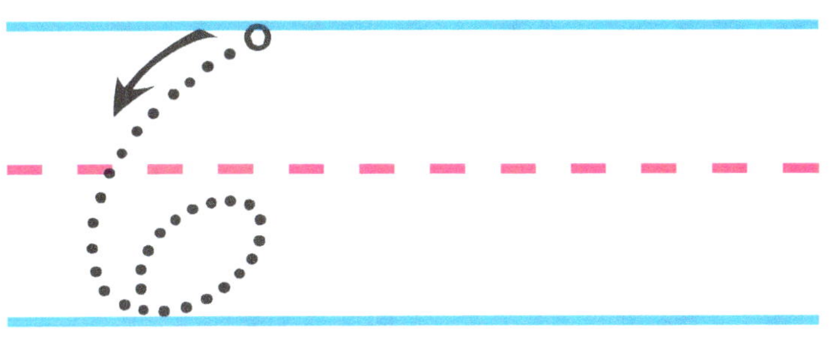

6
six

7

7

seven

7 7 7 7

seven seven seven

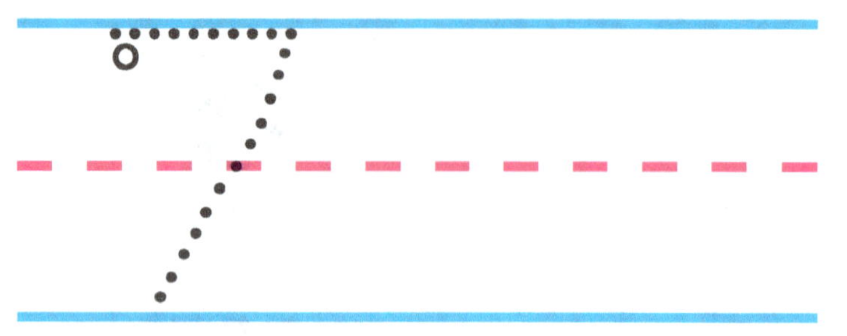

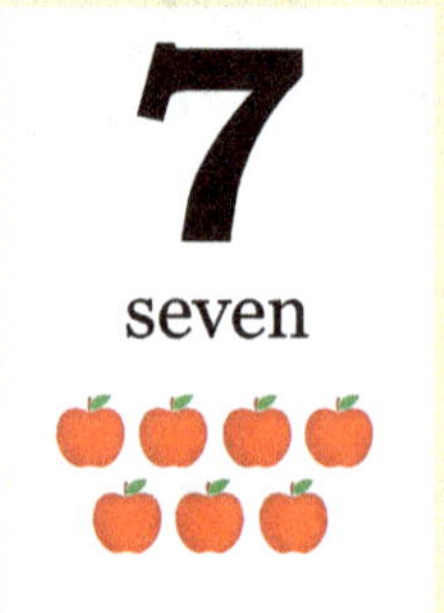

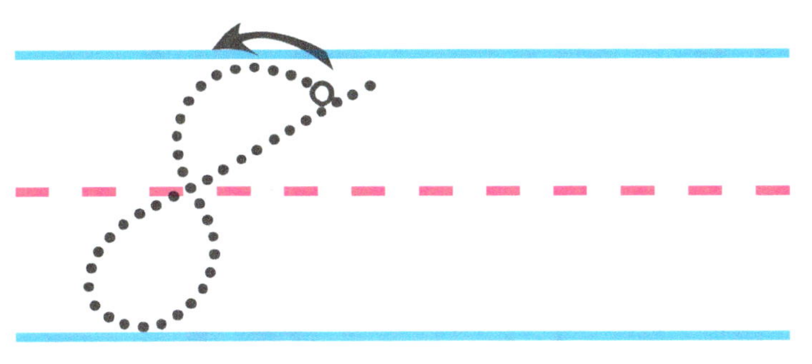

8

eight

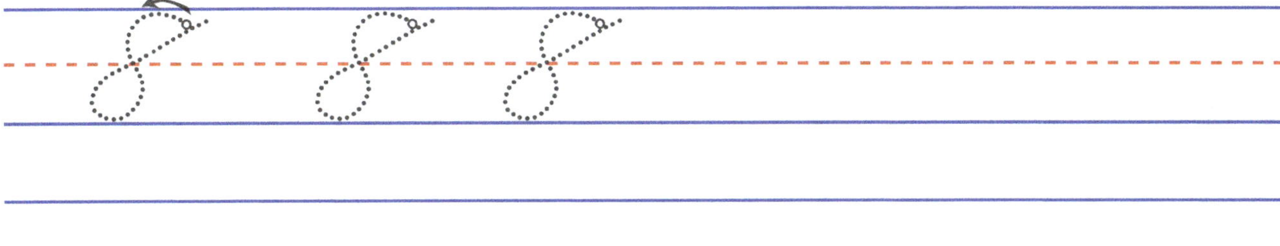

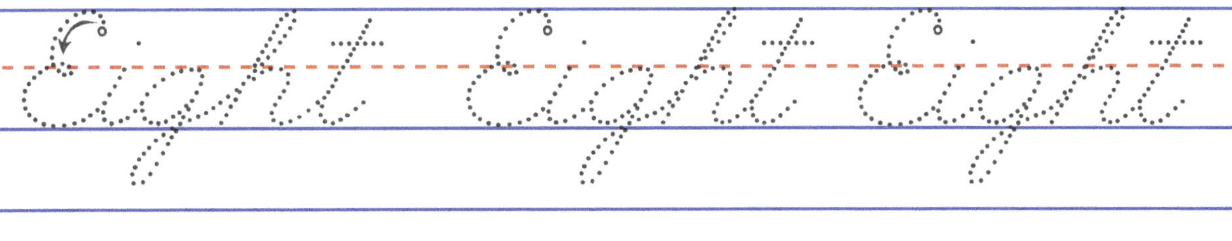

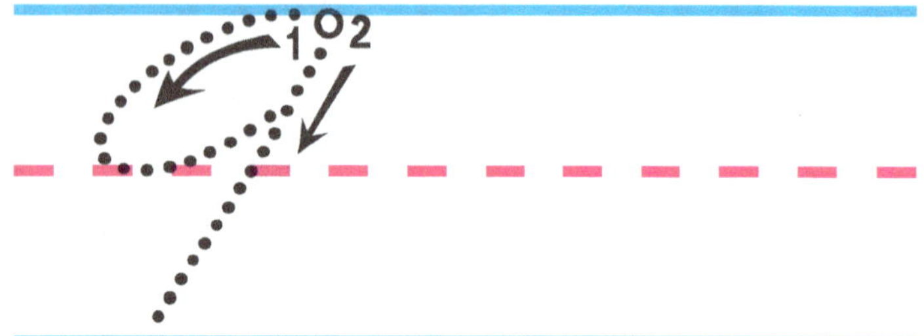

9
nine

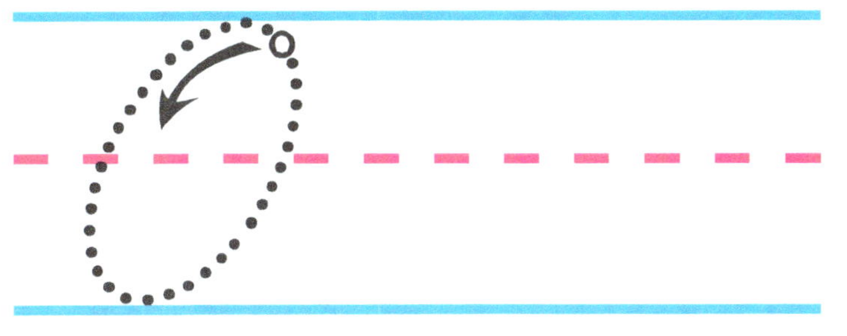

0

zero